Goo Little Brother

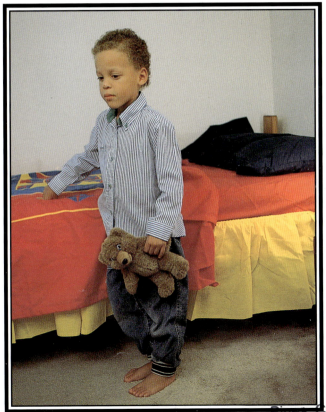

"I don't want to go to bed," said little brother.

"OK," said big sister. "Just put your pajamas on to show Teddy."

"I don't want to go to bed,"
said little brother.

"OK," said big sister.
"Just get under the blankets
to show Teddy."

"I don't want to go to bed," said little brother.

"OK," said big sister. "Just close your eyes to show Teddy."

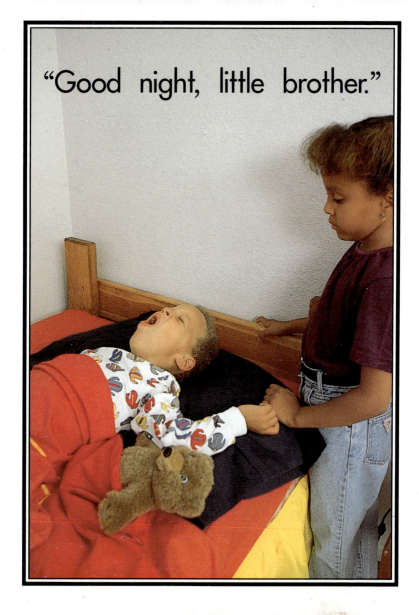

"Good night, little brother."